POETRY
UNDER
OATH

POETRY UNDER OATH

FROM THE TESTIMONY
of
WILLIAM JEFFERSON CLINTON
and
MONICA S. LEWINSKY

Edited by Tom Simon

WORKMAN PUBLISHING · NEW YORK

EDITOR'S NOTE

These are their words, exactly as they were spoken. They have been taken directly from President Clinton's testimony in *Paula Jones v. William Clinton,* and from the President's and Ms. Lewinsky's testimony before Kenneth Starr's Grand Jury.

Transcripts of these sessions abound on the Internet. The page numbers cited in the Index of Titles at the back of this book are from *The Washington Post*'s website (www.washingtonpost.com), with the exception of President Clinton's testimony before Kenneth Starr's Grand Jury, which is from the website of JURIST: The Law Professors' Network (www.jurist.law.pitt.edu).

Selection and adaptation copyright © 1998 Tom Simon.

No portion of this book may be reproduced—mechanically, electronically or by any other means, including photocopying—without written permission of the publisher. Published simultaneously in Canada by Thomas Allen & Son Limited.

ISBN 0-7611-1620-6

Workman books are available at special discounts when purchased in bulk for premium sales promotions as well as for fund-raising or educational use. Special editions or book excerpts can also be created to specification. For details, contact the Special Sales director at the address below.

Workman Publishing Company, Inc.
708 Broadway
New York, NY 10003-9555

Manufactured in the U.S.A.
First printing October 1998
10 9 8 7 6 5 4 3 2 1

CONTENTS

FROM THE TESTIMONY
of W.J.C.

THE OTHERS

VAST CONSPIRACY

FROM THE TESTIMONY
of M.S.L.

FROM THE
TESTIMONY
of
W.J.C.

CHAPTER ONE

Memories, Words & Definitions

The Correct Answer

Let me begin with
The correct answer

I don't know for sure

But if you would like me
To give an educated guess
I will do that

But I do not know for sure

In Ordinary Conversations

If you said Jane
And Harry have
A sexual relationship

And you're not talking
About people being
Drawn into a lawsuit

And being given definitions

And then a great effort
To trick them
In some way

But you are just talking
About people
In ordinary conversations

I'll bet the grand jurors
If they were talking
About two people
They know

And said they have
A sexual relationship

They meant they
Were sleeping together

They meant they
Were having sexual intercourse

For Example, Kissing

I thought the definition
Included any activity by
The person being deposed
Where the person was the actor
And came in contact with
Those parts of the bodies
With the purpose
Or intent of gratification
And excluded
Any other activity

For example
Kissing is not covered by that
I don't think

I Believe It Would

Yes

That would constitute contact
I think that would

If it were direct contact
I believe it would

I—maybe I should
Read it again

Just to make sure

The Lips of Another Person

Because that is—
If the deponent is the person
Who has oral
Sex performed on him

Then the contact is with—
Not with anything on that list
But with the lips
Of another person

It seems to be self-evident
That that's what it is

And I thought it was curious

The Word "Is"

It depends on what
the meaning of the word
"is" is

If the—
if he—
if "is"
means is
and never has been
that is not—

that is one thing

If it means
there is none
that was a

completely
true
statement

Maybe

Oh, no, sir
I don't remember that
Maybe somebody—
Maybe she did

But I only remember—
Well, I don't remember that
That's all I can tell you
I don't remember that

Don't Believe I Do

No sir, I don't
I don't believe I do

I've attempted to look
For any other relevant notes
That might be relevant
To my Counsel or your
Request for discovery

I don't find any
I don't believe I do

No Knowledge of That

I don't think
That question
Ever crossed my mind
One way or the other

I have no knowledge of
That there has been
Any change
In the federal law

If there has been
If there hasn't been

I have no knowledge of that

What I Said

I don't know
That I said that

I don't

I don't remember
What I said

And I don't remember
To whom I said it

The First

I signed it in 1987

And I'm fairly sure that
I was, we were

The first or one of
The very first states

To actually have
A clearly defined

Sexual harassment policy

There Are No Curtains

There are no curtains on the Oval Office
There are no curtains on my private office
There are no curtains or blinds that can close
The windows in my private dining room

The naval aides come and go at will

CHAPTER TWO

"That Woman, Miss Lewinsky"

Around Christmas Time

I did like it a lot
I told you that

My impression
My belief
Was that she gave me that book
For Christmas

Maybe that's not right

I think she had that book
Delivered to me
For Christmas

And then
As I remember
I went to Bosnia

And for some reason
She wasn't there
Around Christmas time

Basically a Good Girl

She's basically a good girl

She's a good young woman
With a good heart
And a good mind

I think she is burdened
By some unfortunate conditions
Of her, her upbringing

But she's basically a good person

In Most of These Cards

Most of them were signed
"Love"
You know
"Love, Monica"

I don't know that
I would consider—

I don't believe that
In most of these cards
And letters she professed
Her love

But she might well have

If I Could

And did I want
If I could
To avoid talking
About Monica Lewinsky?

Yes

I'd give anything
In the world
Not to be here
Talking about it

I'd be giving—
I'd give anything
In the world
Not to have to admit
What I've had to admit
Today

But . . .

The Other Thing

She may have felt some ambivalence
About how to react
Because there were some times
When she seemed to say
Yes
When I'm not sure she meant
Yes

There was a time—
It seems like
There was one
Or two
Things where she said
Well, remember
This, that

Or the other thing

Which did reflect
My recollection
So I would say a little yes
And a little no

In the Context of Her Desire

She raised the issue with me
In the context of her desire
To avoid testifying

Which I certainly understood

Not only because there were
Some embarrassing facts
About our relationship

That were inappropriate

But also because a whole lot
Of innocent people were
Being traumatized
And dragged
Through the mud
By these Jones
Lawyers
With their
Dragnet
Strategy

It's Possible

Yes, that's correct

It's possible
That she . . .
While she
Was working there

Brought something
To me and
That at the time
She brought it to me

She was the only person there

That's possible

Pizza

At some point during the government
shutdown
when Ms. Lewinsky was still
an intern

But was working the chief staff's
office
because all the employees had to
go home . . .

She was back there with
a pizza
that she brought to me and
to others

I do not believe she was there
alone

Sunday Afternoon

Now

The next time I remember
Seeing her alone
Was on a couple of occasions

When she was working
In the Legislative Affairs Office
As a full-time employee

I remember specifically
I have a specific recollection
Of two times

I don't remember when they were

But I remember twice when
On Sunday afternoon
She brought papers down to me

Stayed

And we were alone

When We Were Alone

But there were also
A lot of times when
Even though no one could see us

The doors were open

To the halls
One on both ends
Of the halls

People could hear

The Navy stewards
Could come in and out
At will

If they were around

Other things could be happening
So there were a lot of times
When we were alone

But I never really thought we were

That Day

I knew that at some point

I don't know whether I found out
That, that day

I knew that day

I knew that
Somehow she knew . . .
That Eleanor Mondale
Was in

To see us that day

I knew that
I don't know
That I knew
How she knew that

On that day

I don't remember that

New York

It became obvious that
You know

Her mother had moved to New York
She wanted to go to New York

She wasn't going to get a job in the White House

A Friend of Betty

You know
She was a—

She had worked
In the White House
She had worked
In the Defense Department
And she was moving
To New York

She was a friend of Betty

The Right Thing

It may be

That when I did the right thing
And made it stick
That in a way she felt a need
To cling more closely

Or try to get closer
To me

Even though she knew
Nothing improper
Was happening or
Was going to happen

I don't know the answer to that

And I Never Asked Her to Lie

I can tell you this:
I never asked Ms. Lewinsky to lie . . .

I told her
she had
to get
a lawyer

And I never asked her to lie . . .

I can tell you this:
In the context of whether she
could be a witness
I have a recollection that she
asked me, well, what do I do
if I get called as a witness

And I said
you have
to get
a lawyer

And that's all I said
And I never asked her to lie

Never

No . . .

It's certainly not the truth
It would not be the truth

. . . I have never
Had sexual relations
With Monica Lewinsky

I've never had
An affair
With her

CHAPTER THREE

The Others

Kathleen

1.

When I heard
That he was dead
And that he apparently
Killed himself

I called her
And expressed my condolences
And said she could take whatever
Time she needed

It was a brief call

2.

When she came to see me
She was clearly upset

I did to her
What I have done
To scores and scores
Of men and women
Who have worked for me
Or been my friends
Over the years

I embraced her
I put
My arms around her
I may have even
Kissed her
On the forehead

3.

The meeting I recall
Occurred before
Her husband's death . . .

My recollection is
That she requested
Several times
To come in to see me

She wanted to come in
And see me
And kept asking to do that

And my—
And she did come in
To see me

He Was a Friend of Mine Too

The fact that her husband
Was not there
Was incidental

She was a friend of mine

And I would go by
And see her
From time to time

I hadn't been visiting
with her in a long time

Sometimes I saw him
When she wasn't there

He was a friend of mine
Too

Betty

I told Betty
Currie not to worry . . .
That she had been through a terrible time

She had lost her brother
She had lost her sister
Her mother was in the hospital

I said, Betty
Just don't worry about me
Just relax
Go in there and tell the truth

You'll be fine

For a Minute or Two

I believe
This was in the lobby
Of the Quapaw tower

But

It could have been
On the floor
Where her apartment was

And if so

I could have
Stuck my head in there
For a minute or two

But I don't believe so

CHAPTER FOUR

Vast Conspiracy

Paranoia

After I went through a presidential campaign
In which the far right tried
To convince the American people I had

Committed murder
Run drugs
Slept in my mother's bed
With four prostitutes
And done numerous other things

I had a high level of paranoia

What Was Going On

I'm trying
To be honest with you
And it hurts me

And I'm trying
To tell you
The truth

About what happened
Between Ms. Lewinsky
And me

But that does not
Change the fact that
The real reason they
Were zeroing in on
Anybody

Was to try to get
Any person in there

No matter how uninvolved
With Paula Jones

No matter how uninvolved
With sexual harassment

So they could hurt me
Politically

That's what was going on

I Wanted to Be Legal

In the face of that
I knew

That in the face
Of their illegal activity
I still had to behave

Lawfully

I wanted to be legal
Without being
Particularly helpful

I thought

That was
That was what
I was trying to do

In the End

What I remember is
There were two different
Discussions . . .
And everybody was
Entering into it

And in the end
The Judge said that she would
Take the first definition
And strike the rest of it

That's my memory . . .

And in the end
The Judge says
"I'm talking only about
Part one in the definition"
And "Do you understand that?"

And I answer
"I do."

What They Wanted

What they wanted to do
And what they did do
And what they had done
By the time I showed up here

Was to find any negative information
They could on me
Whether it was true or not
Get it in a deposition

And then leak it
Even though
It was illegal
To do so

It happened
Repeatedly

The Judge gave them orders

Off the Wall

Because these questions were—
Some of them were
Off the wall
Some of them were
Way out of line
I thought

And what I wanted to establish
Was that Betty was there . . .
And I wanted to know
What Betty's memory was
About what she heard
What she could hear

And what I did not know was—
I did not know that

And I was trying to figure out

And I was trying to figure out
In a hurry because I knew

Something was up

With Such Conviction

Mr. Fisher
Is there something
Let me just—

You asked that
With such conviction
And I answered
With such conviction

Is there something
You want to ask me
About this?

. . . I don't even know
What you're talking about

I don't think

No Recollection

I don't think I have
Any other notes

I've tried to find
Any notes
That would be responsive
To your request
For production

We've given you some
Other notes that I have
. . . I don't think
I have any more

And I have no recollection
Of taking any

All These Women

Oh, yes, sir
She was upset
She—
Well, she—we
She didn't—we didn't talk

About a subpoena

But she was upset
She said, I don't want
To testify
I know nothing
About this . . .

And I explained to her

Why they were doing this
And why all these women
Were on these lists

You Would Qualify

We were joking
About how you-all
With the help of

The Rutherford Institute

Were going to call
Every woman I'd
Ever talked to . . .

And I said

That you-all might call
Every woman I
Ever talked to

And ask them that

And so I said
You would qualify

Or something like that

Shut the Government Down

There was a period
When . . .
The Republican Congress
Shut the government down
That the whole White House

Was being run by interns

All I'm Saying

All I'm saying is . . .
Let me say
Something sympathetic
To you

I've been pretty tough
So, let me say
Something sympathetic:

All of you are intelligent people

I Think I Have Been

I think I have been
Quite specific and
I think I've been

Willing to answer
Some specific questions
That I haven't been
Asked yet

But I do not want
To discuss something
That is intensely painful
To me

This has been
Tough enough already
On me and on my family

Although I take
Responsibility for it

I have no one
to blame but myself

CHAPTER FIVE

Gifts

One Other Thing

I don't remember
That . . .
I just don't remember

I remember
Giving her the Bear
And the Throw
I don't remember what else

And it seems to me
There was one other thing
In that bag

I didn't remember the cherry chocolates

I Get These Ties

Yes

She had given me
A tie before
I believe that's right

Now, as I said
Let me remind you
Normally, when
I get these ties

I get ties
You know, together
And they're given
To me later

But I believe
That she
Has given me a tie

Gifts All the Time

You know
The President gets hundreds of gifts a year
Maybe more

I have always
Given a lot of gifts to people
Especially if they give me gifts

And this was no big deal to me

I mean, it's nice
I enjoy it
I gave dozens of personal gifts to people
Last Christmas

I give gifts to people all the time
Friends of mine give me gifts all the time

Give me ties
Give me books
Give me other things

So, it was just not a big deal

A Lot of Those Cards

She sent cards sometimes
That were just
Funny
Even a little bit
Off-color

But they were funny

She liked
To send me cards
And I got a lot of those cards

Several, anyway

I don't know a lot
I got a few

To Be a Friend

I had
For nearly a year
Done my best
To be a friend to Ms. Lewinsky

To be a counselor to her
To give her good advice
And to help her

She had
For her part
Most of the time accepted
The changed circumstances

She talked to me a lot
About her life
Her job, her ambitions

And she continued to give me gifts
And I felt that it was a right thing to do

To give her gifts back

FROM THE
TESTIMONY
of
M.S.L.

CHAPTER SIX

The President

In the Back Office

Because I believe it was—
It was really more the president
Choosing the hallway
I think, and it was—
There weren't any windows there
It was the most secluded
Of all the places
In the back office

Well, that's not true
The bathroom is the most
Secluded, I guess

Because you can close the door

Little Tiny Spot

I told him
That I really cared about him

And he told me
That he didn't want to get
Addicted to me
And he didn't want me to get
Addicted to him
And we embraced at that point

And that's—
I mean, it was—it's just a

Little tiny spot
Down here

And a
Little tiny spot
Up here

Oh, No

Yes

And at that point
I noticed it
And I kind of thought, oh
This is dirty

It needs to get cleaned

And then I remembered
That I had worn it
The last time
I saw the president

And I believe it was
At that point that
I thought to myself
Oh, no

There Was Always Kissing

I think the only thing
That might be missing

Is kissing . . .

I mean

Because
The physical intimacy—

Wherever
There's physical intimacy

There was always—
There was always

Kissing

With His Eyes Wide Open

December 28th of last year . . .
I was getting my Christmas kiss
And he was kissing me in the doorway
Between the back study
Or the office
And the hallway

And I sort of opened my eyes
And he was looking out the window
With his eyes wide open
While he was kissing me
And then I got mad
Because it wasn't very romantic
And then so then he said

"Well, I
Was just looking
To see

To make sure
No one was
Out there"

At His Age

He didn't want to

The president said that he—
That at his age
That there was too much
Of a consequence

In doing that

And that when I
Got to be his age
I would understand

But I wasn't happy
With that

Pizza

And when the pizza came
I went down
To let him know
That the pizza was there . . .

I said I needed to pack
And he said, "Well, why don't
You bring me some pizza?"

So I asked him
If he wanted
Vegetable
Or meat

I Made an Effort

I'm an insecure person
And so I think—

And I was insecure
About the relationship
At times and thought

That he would come
To forget me easily

And if I hadn't
Heard from him—
Especially after I
Left the White House

It was—it was very
Difficult for me

I always liked to see him . . .
And usually when I'd see him
It would kind of prompt
Him to call me

So I made an effort

I would go early
And stand in front
So I could see him

Blah, blah, blah

If It Got Lost

There were on some occasions
When I sent him cards or notes . . .
I wrote things that he deemed too personal
To put on paper just in case

Something ever happened

If it got lost getting there
Or someone else opened it

So there were several times
When he remarked to me
You know, you shouldn't put that
On paper

Sunshine

We would tell jokes
We would talk about our childhoods
Talk about current events

I was always giving him
My stupid ideas
About what I thought should be done
In the administration or
Different views on things

I think back on it
And he always made me smile
When I was with him

It was a lot of—
He was sunshine

Call Me When You're Alone

I don't know if inappropriate
Is the right word

I—there were very few
Discussions and I tended
To say things like

"Well, when you're alone"
You know
"Call me when you're alone"

. . . That was how
We discussed sort of
Mrs. Clinton maybe not
Being there . . .

"Well, I'll be alone
On this day
Shall I—"

I think we were careful—
Or I was careful

I know I was

He Was Just Angry

And he was just angry with me
And he told me it was none of my business
What—you know
What he was doing . . .
He had never been treated as poorly
By anyone else as I treated him
And that he spent more time
With me
Than anyone else
In the world

Aside from his family
Friends and staff . . .

I didn't know exactly which
Category that put me in

I Started Crying

Yes
Our meeting started out
With a fight

So he sat down
And we sat down
And he lectured me . . .
"First of all, it's illegal
To threaten the President
Of the United States
And, second of all—"
I mean, it was just—

And then I started crying

Like That

He told me that he thought
That my being transferred
Had something to do with him
And that he was upset
He said

"Why
Do they have to
Take you away
From me?

I trust you"

And then he told me—
He looked at me
And he said

"I promise you
If I win in November
I'll bring you back

Like that"

Really Upset

Okay

I asked him how—
If he was doing okay
With Ron Brown's death

And then after we talked
About that for a little bit
I told him that

My last day was Monday
And he was—
He seemed really upset

More Bad News

And he told me
That he had two things
To tell me. The first

Was that Betty's brother
Had been killed
In a car accident . . .
The same brother who
Had been beaten up
Just a few months ago
And she had lost her sister
And her mom was ill

We talked about Betty
For a little bit
And then he told me
He had some more
Bad news, that he had
Seen the witness list
For the Paula Jones case

And my name was on it

Vanilla Subpoena

When I mentioned to him
I think, about the hat pin
He said, "Oh,
Don't worry about it

This is a vanilla subpoena
This is a standard subpoena"

Something like that
Generic subpoena, maybe . . .

Well, what I understood
That to mean was that—

That what he was trying
To say is there was nothing
Out of the ordinary about
This subpoena

The Untrue Statements

Yes

There were some truths
In December of '97

There certainly were
Some true statements

But

There were a lot of
Untrue statements

Probably the untrue statements
Stick out in my mind more

Because they caused so much trouble

CHAPTER SEVEN

The Others

Mr. Ickes

You would pass Mr. Ickes
In the hall
And he would just glare at you
You know

And I'd say, "Hello"
You know
As you would imagine
You're supposed to do

And he'd just glare at you
And walk past you
And I thought
That was strange

Call me weird

Mr. Jordan

Yes

After breakfast, in the car
I asked Mr. Jordan
If he thought the President
Would always be married

To the First Lady

And he said, "Yes
As he should be"
And gave me a quote
From the Bible

And a few—
Maybe a minute or so later
He said, "Well
Maybe you two will have an affair

When he's out of office . . ."

And I said, "Well
We already had an affair

We just—
You know
We didn't have sex
Or did everything but sex"

Or something like that

And he just kind of went
One of those

"Mmmph"

A Crime in Washington

I'm a friendly person

And—
And I didn't know
It was a crime
In Washington

For people—for you
To want people to like you

And so I was friendly

And I guess
I wasn't
Supposed to be

I Just Went In

It was John Muskett, I believe
And I had brought some papers
With me from home
And so I believe I said something
"Oh, the President asked me to
Bring these to him"
And John Muskett said
"Oh, I'd better check with
Evelyn Lieberman"
And I don't remember exactly
What the rest of the exchange was

But

I talked him out of doing
that and
then I
just
went
in

Linda

1.

I was very nervous

I was wary
Of her
I actually thought
She might have
A tape recorder
With her

And had looked
In her bag
When she had gone
Up to the restroom

I told her
A whole bunch of lies
That day

2.

I told her
I didn't yet have a job
That wasn't true

I told her
I hadn't signed the affidavit
That wasn't true

I told her
That some time
Over the holidays

I had freaked out
And my mom took me
To Georgetown Hospital
And they put me
On Paxil
That wasn't true

3.

I didn't learn the extent
To which she had taped
My conversations

Until I read it in the press

I learned that day
That she had worn
A wire at the lunch

And that I—
And that there

Had been other people
I think
In the restaurant
That had been listening in
And—

So I knew—

She had—
She had said that—
That—when I was
First apprehended

She was—
She had said that
They had done
The same thing to her

And she tried to hug me

And she told me
This was the best thing
For me to do

And—oh

They Had Me on Tape

And they told me . . .

They knew that I had
Signed a false affidavit
They had me on tape

Saying I had committed perjury
That they were going to—
That I could go to jail

For 27 years

They were going
To charge me with perjury

And obstruction of justice
And subornation of perjury
And witness tampering

And something else

I Would Just Like to Say

I would just like to say

That no one ever
Asked me to lie

And I was never
Promised a job
For my silence

And that I'm sorry
I'm really sorry
For everything that's happened

And I hate Linda Tripp

Blab, Blab, Blab

"Bob Nash is handling it"
"Marsha's going to handle it"
And "We just sort of need to be careful"

You know
And "Oh, I'll—"
He would always sort of—

What's the word I'm looking for?

Kind of validate
What I was feeling
By telling me something
That I don't necessarily know
Is true

"Oh, I'll talk to her"
"I'll—you know, I'll see
blah, blah, blah"

And it was just
"I'll do," "I'll do," "I'll do"
And didn't, didn't, didn't . . .

CHAPTER EIGHT

Gifts

Another Time

Oh

Our meeting ended up—
Or was cut short
By the fact
That he had to have
A meeting with Mr. Bowles

So

He told me
That he'd give me
My Christmas present
Another time and

That he wouldn't
Jerk me
Around and
Abandon me

Let Betty Be

He said he'd try
And see if Betty
Could come in
On the weekend

To give me my Christmas presents

And I told him
That was out
Of the question
To—you know

Let Betty be

(Q: Because her brother had just
been killed, right?
A: Right.)

Because If He Is

Then one of the guards
Said, "Oh, are you here
To see Betty Currie?"
And I said, "No . . .
She doesn't know I'm coming"

And then they told me . . .
She was giving a tour to
Eleanor Mondale

Then I sort of—

wanting to know
if the President was
in the office

Asked the guards:
"Oh, well, is the President
In the office?
Because if he is
She's probably too busy
To come out
And get these gifts"

Goofing Off

Betty and the President and I
Were in the Oval Office
And this was the first time
I got to meet Buddy

So we played with Buddy
In the office
And he was running
Around the carpet

And I had brought a small
Christmas present for Buddy
And so the three of us
Were just talking

And goofing off

And then the President
And I went
Into the back study

And he gave me my
Christmas presents

And So I Love Ties

I don't know if
You all know this or not

But I worked
In a men's necktie store
When I was in college
For four years

And so that was my thing . . .

My spending money
A lot of it came from working
And so I love ties

And I, I mean, I can pick out—
You know—
Different designers and stuff

And so that was a big thing for me

My Gifts

A tie

A mug
from Starbucks
in Santa Monica

A little box
That's called hugs
And kisses
And it's Xs and Os inside
It's really—
It's just a cute little tchotchke

An antique book
from the flea market
in New York
that was on Theodore Roosevelt

And—I think that's it

In the Back Study

I lent him the book
"Disease and Misrepresentation" . . .
I saw it in the back study

. . . And then the letter opener
That I was mentioning
A moment ago . . .

It was on top of—
I think it's a cigar box
On his desk

In the back office

INDEX OF TITLES/SOURCES

Note: Figures following the names in parentheses refer to website page numbers; those preceding the names refer to part numbers.
JVC = *Jones v. Clinton*, January 17, 1998 (www.washingtonpost.com)
STARR = Testimony before Kenneth Starr's Grand Jury: WJC, August 17, 1998 (www.jurist.law.pitt.edu.); MSL, August 6* and 20** (see Post URL above)